EYE TO EYE WITH HORSES

Arabian Horses

Lynn M. Stone

Rourke
Publishing LLC
Vero Beach, Florida 32964

www.rourkepublishing.com

PHOTO CREDITS: All photos © Lynn M. Stone except for pages 5 and 11 courtesy of Astrid and Gerhard Skorianz, photographers and producers of the documentary motion picture Children of the Wind, www.kinderdeswindes.com

Editor: Robert Stengard-Olliges

Cover and page design by Tara Raymo

Library of Congress Cataloging-in-Publication Data

Stone, Lynn M.
 Arabian horses / Lynn Stone.
    p. cm. -- (Eye to eye with horses)
 ISBN 978-1-60044-581-1
 1. Arabian horse--Juvenile literature. I. Title.
 SF293.A8S76 2008
 636.1'12--dc22
                                        2007019085

Printed in the USA

CG/CG

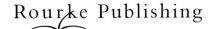

Rourke Publishing

www.rourkepublishing.com – rourke@rourkepublishing.com
Post Office Box 3328, Vero Beach, FL 32964

Table of Contents

Arabian Horses

Imagine sharing a tent with a horse! It would have to be a very important horse, wouldn't it?

For the Bedouin tribes of old Arabia, nothing was more important than their horses. The horses transported them on raids and into warfare, often against other Bedouins. Their horses were also objects of great religious importance in the Islamic faith. And the horses, along with camels, helped the **nomadic** tribes move across the desert sands. From time to time, a Bedouin's tent became a shelter for a Bedouin's horse.

The Arabian horse was closely tied to the Bedouins' Islamic religious beliefs.

A beautiful Arabian rests in the shade under a tree.

Graceful, modern Arabs are much like their ancestors of the Middle East deserts.

Bedouin horses are now known as Arabians. Amazingly, modern Arabians, sometimes called Arabs, aren't much different from their ancestors. Arabians have always been beautiful horses.

ARABIAN FACTS

The Arabian is one of the most popular breeds in the world.

Arabians are a very popular breed. Arabians are bred and loved on every continent except Antarctica!

The old breed welcomes a new member in Florida.

Arabians have been bred pure—apart from other **breeds**—for at least 1,000 years. That makes the Arabian the oldest horse breed in the world. It is also the breed with the most impact on other breeds.

The History of Arabian Horses

The Arabian horse of the Bedouins came from the Arabian peninsula. The fierce, private Bedouins had little interest in the "outside world." They kept their society and their hardy desert horses largely to themselves. The Bedouins treasured their horses. They wanted no part of mixing their horses with other breeds.

*Arab riders race their horses through a tent camp in
the desert.*

One for me, one for you: A gentle Arabian and a child share horse kibbles.

Born in the desert and carefully raised, an Arabian horse became both tough and gentle. And it showed great endurance—an ability to keep going where and when other horses would have died. That combination of gentleness and strength remains in Arabian horses today.

By the 16th century, Europeans had seen several Arabian type horses. These "horses from the East" had great value for warfare. They were smaller and faster than European breeds, yet they had endurance. By the 19th century, Europe had begun raising its own Arabians.

A very few Arabian horses first showed up in North America in the 1700's. Americans raised a few Arabians in the mid-1800's. The first big import of Arabian horses to America was in 1906. Homer Davenport was allowed to bring 27 horses directly from the Arabian desert.

Arabians can run further at speed than Thoroughbreds.

Arabian horses were used to help refine the Thoroughbred breed (shown here).

The Thoroughbred didn't have the Arabian's endurance, but it was faster on a mile-long race track. Some breeders mixed Arabians with Thoroughbreds in order to make a better Thoroughbred. Arabians were also used to develop or improve Percherons, Morgans, and many other breeds.

Being an Arabian Horse

Arabian horses should have large eyes and a short, slightly dipped back. Many Arabians have a distinct "dished" face. Some Arabians are **selectively bred** for that particular feature. But don't count on a **purebred** Arabian having a dished face.

Large eyes, dished face, and graceful, arched neck are typical of many Arabian horses.

A rider works out her high-stepping Arabian horse.

An Arabian trots with style, like it is bouncing off springs. It shows a high, arched neck and flowing tail. Arabians have a different bone formation in their ribs, back, and tail than other breeds. That helps explain the high **carriage** of their tails.

An alert Arabian in the evening sun.

An Arabian horse's silky coat shines in the late afternoon.

Arabians have a deep, broad chest and a silky coat over black skin. The coat may be chestnut, gray, bay, or black. Some have white markings, usually on the face or legs.

An Arabian may be taller than 15 **hands** high, but it is usually around 14.3 hands.

Owning an Arabian Horse

Perhaps more than any other breed, Arabians usually have a gentle, curious, and even friendly spirit. Like a golden retriever, an Arabian mare may demand a good scratching. As in any breed, however, stallions may be difficult to handle.

A trainer exercises an Arabian horse on a long rope.

While having its hoof trimmed, an Arabian horse gently nuzzles the farrier.

Because Arabians thrive on contact with humans, they need a lot of attention. The Arab is not a good choice of breeds if the owner has little time for the animal.

Arabs are **versatile** horses. Some are entered in **conformation** shows. Some are used in races against other Arabs. Some are entered in long-distance, endurance rides. Arabs are also trail, jumping, and **dressage** horses.

High-spirited Arabian stallion gallops in a California pasture.

Glossary

breed (BREED) – a group of domestic animals within a group (such as Arabians among horses) having the same basic characteristics

carriage (KA rij) – the way an animal carries itself

conformation (kuhn for MAY shuhn) – an animal's body shape and size

dressage (dres SAHge) – complicated movements by a horse in reaction to a rider's shifting weight

hand (HAND) – a 4-inch (10 centimeter) unit to measure the height to a horse's shoulder

nomadic (NO maa dik) – to move from place to place

purebred (PUR BRED) – a domestic animal of a single breed, such as a purebred Arabian horse

selectively bred (si LEK tiv lee BRED) – an animal whose parents were carefully chosen

versatile (VUR suh tuhl) – able to do many things well

Index

Further Reading

Braulick, Carrie A. *The Arabian Horse*. Capstone, 2005.

Dell, Pamela. *Arabians*. Child's World, 2007.

Henry, Marguerite. *King of the Wind*. DIANE Publishing, 2005.

Website to Visit

www.arabianhorses.org

www.waho.org

About the Author

Lynn M. Stone is the author of more than 400 children's books. He is a talented natural history photographer as well. Lynn, a former teacher, travels worldwide to photograph wildlife in its natural habitat.